THE SENSES OF SMELL AND TASTE ARE BEST FRIENDS!

Biology 1st Grade

Children's Biology Books

Speedy Publishing LLC
40 E. Main St. #1156
Newark, DE 19711
www.speedypublishing.com

In this book, we're going to talk about the sense of smell and taste and how they work together. So, let's get right to it!

There are cinnamon rolls baking in the oven and you can smell them. You go outdoors and someone is burning leaves in their backyard and you can smell them. You pluck a rose from the garden and smell it. It smells wonderful, but some pollen gets up your nose and it makes you sneeze! A light breeze blows around you and you breathe in the fresh, cool air. Your nose helps you breathe and smell.

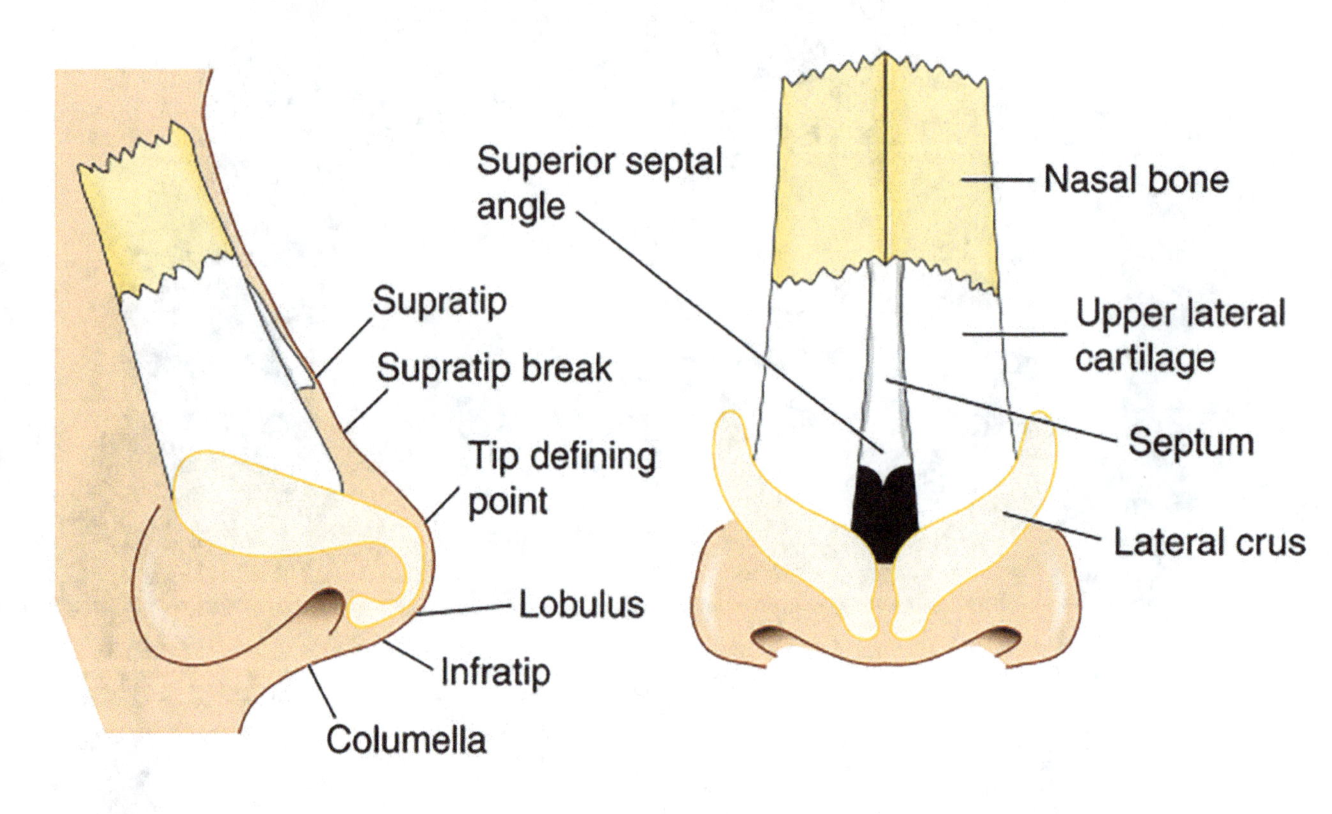

Anatomy of the Nose

THE STRUCTURE OF THE NOSE

There are thousands of different shapes of noses, but no matter what shape nose you have, your nose has two nasal passages on the inside and two openings that are called nostrils. The two passages have a septum that separates them from each other. Sometimes, if you have a cold, one side of your nose is clogged and the other isn't.

At the tip of your nose, the septum is cartilage instead of bone. If you push on the end of your nose you can make it move a little left and right. The septum continues from the tip of your nose to the bridge of your nose to your skull. Your nose has a foundation of bone behind it and also at the top going into the skull.

You use your nose for lots of different reasons. You use it to smell. You use it to help you breathe. You also use it as a filter to keep out things that shouldn't go in your lungs. Your nose warms the air that travels through it and moistens it before it goes down into your lungs.

If you've ever seen a picture of a skull, you know that behind the nose is a space. That space is the nasal cavity and it connects to the back of your throat. It's also separated from the interior of your mouth by the roof on the inside of your mouth, which is called the palate.

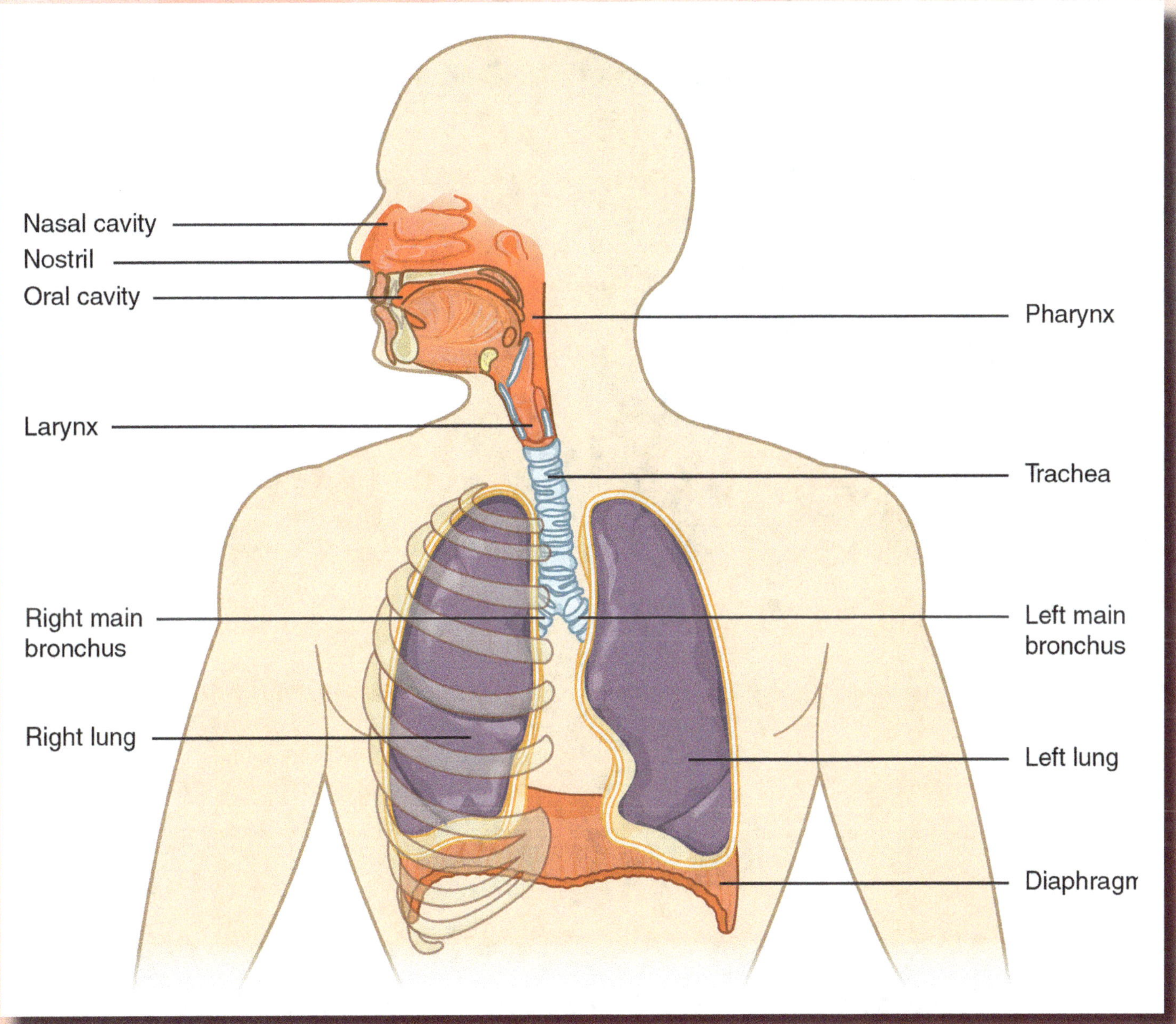

Major Respiratory Organs

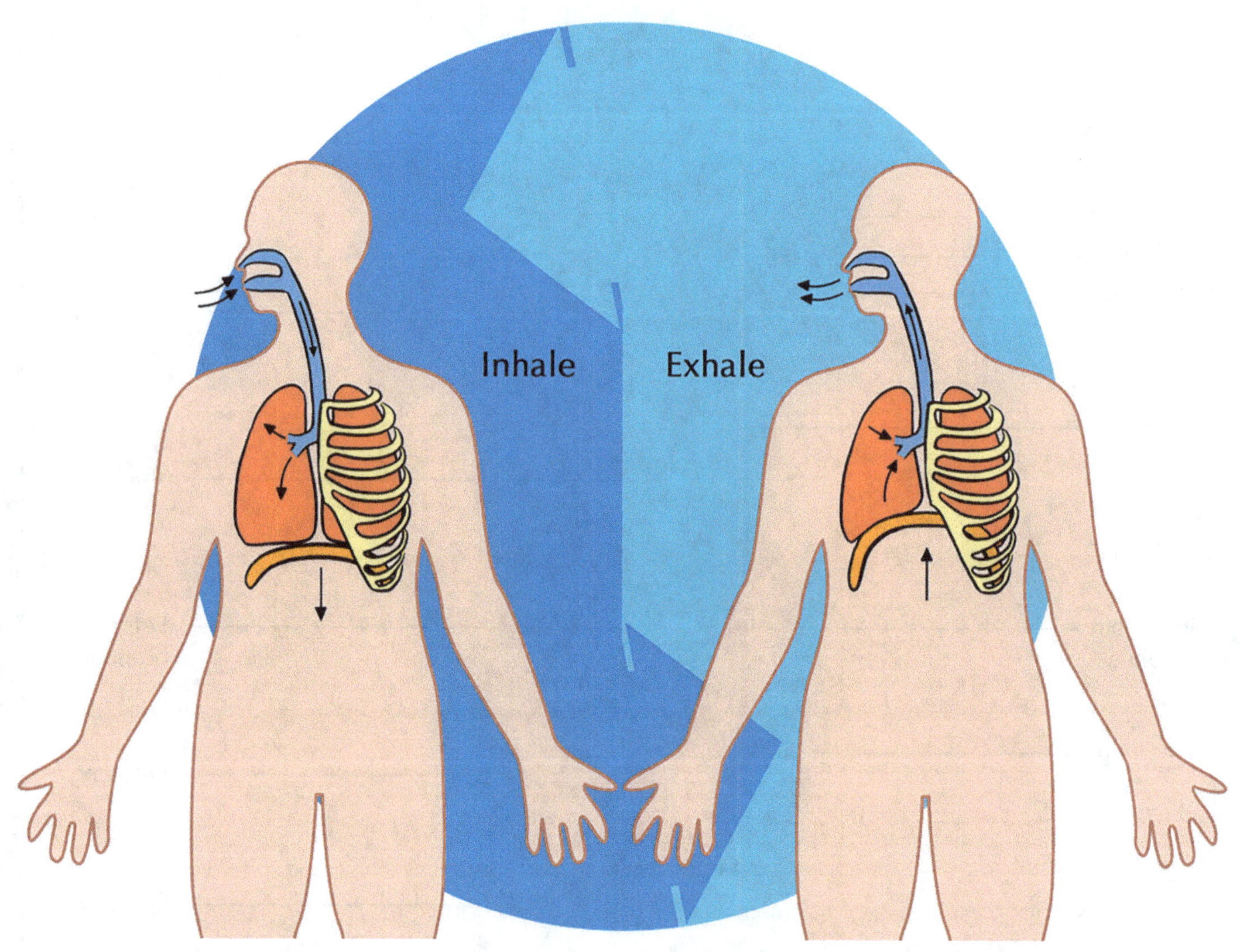

Inhalation and exhalation are the processes by which the body brings in oxygen and releases carbon dioxide.

HOW DO YOU BREATHE WITH YOUR NOSE?

When you breathe, air travels up through your open nostrils and up through your nasal passages. Your nose prepares the air to make it feel good inside your lungs.

It warms it up and it makes it a little wetter. Also, if there are some particles of dust or something else that could irritate your lungs, the mucous membrane in your nose creates mucus that captures those. The mucus is a sticky white substance that you might call snot.

The air that goes into your lungs is cleaner thanks to your nose. When you clean out or blow your nose, those impurities will go out. If you sneeze, the particles come flying out, sometimes at speeds of over 100 miles per hour! Some will go down your throat into your stomach, but that's okay because your stomach can process out that waste better than your lungs can.

The air goes in through your nose or mouth or both, so that you can get oxygen that you need to live. The waste product of air, carbon dioxide, goes out through your nose and mouth as well.

HOW DO YOU SMELL WITH YOUR NOSE?

In order to smell something, like the cinnamon rolls in the oven, molecules from those objects have to travel in the air to the inside of your nose. Some things have smells, but others don't. For example, an onion has a pungent smell, but a piece of stainless steel like a fork doesn't have a smell at all. In the back of your nose, there is an area about the size of a postage stamp that processes the smells.

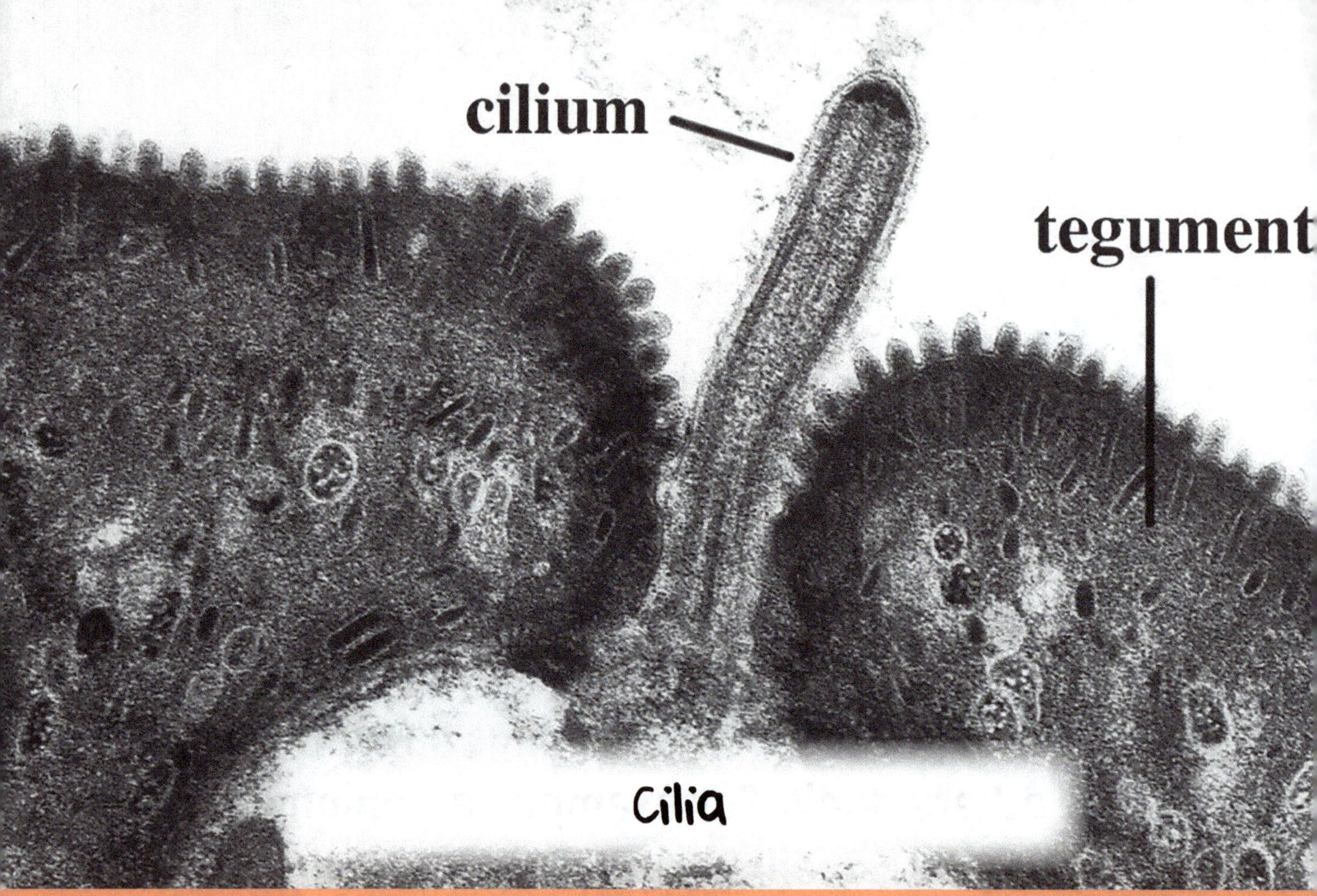

Cilia are very tiny hairs inside your nose. They are not like the hairs you can see. These hairs are so tiny, they can only be seen with a

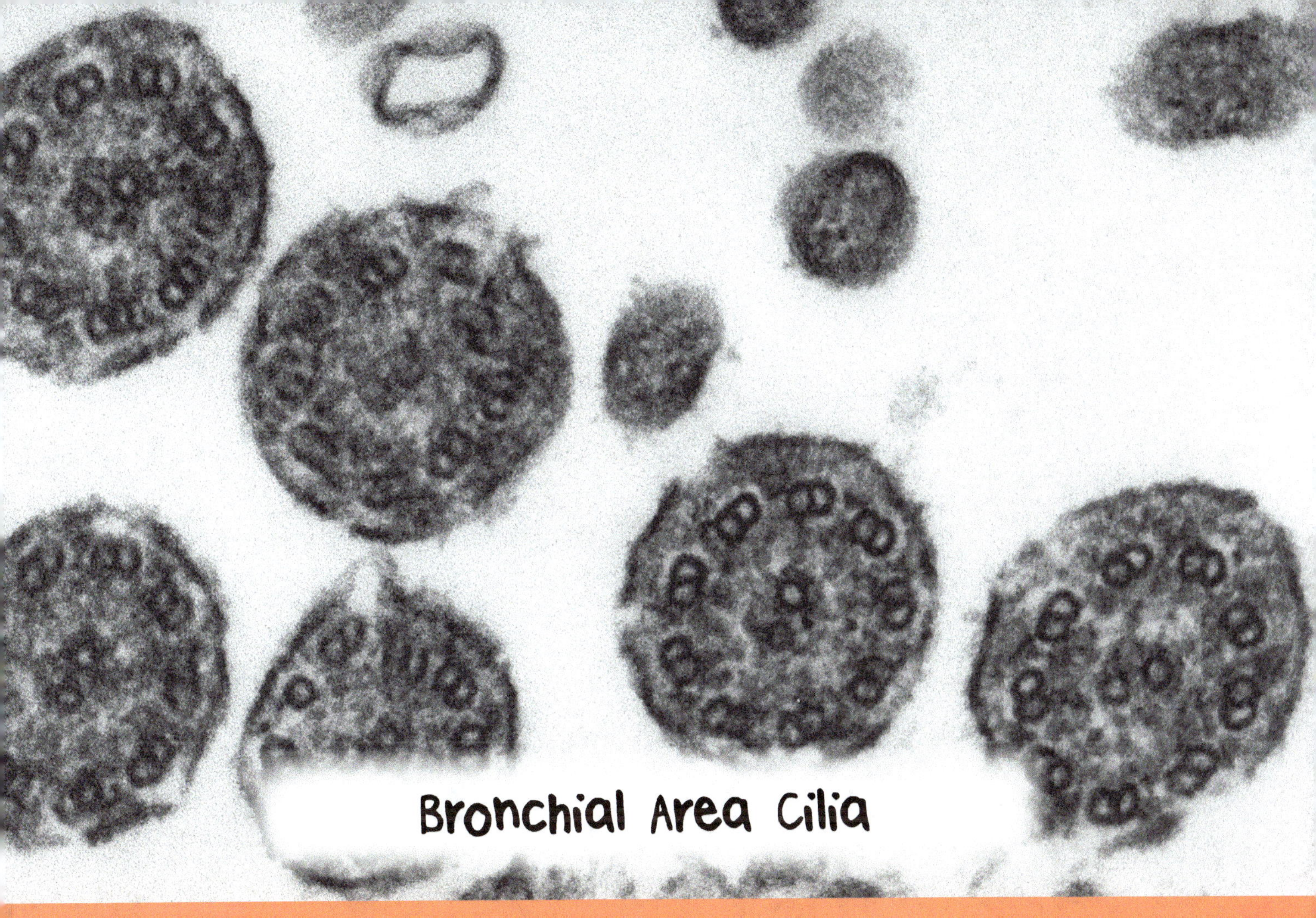

microscope. There are millions of them and they are on the surface of this "postage-stamp-sized" area.

They capture the molecules of the smell and that triggers the neurons. The neurons are special nerves that will help your brain figure out what it's smelling. That's why we sniff to smell things. That way we can get more of the molecules into the part of our noses that help us smell.

DIFFERENT SMELLS

There are more than 10,000 different smells you can identify with your nose, but, for the most part, the smells you smell fall into ten different categories.

- Citrus smells, like lemon juice or a lime picked off a tree
- Fruity smells, like berries, pears, and apples

Citrus smell

Relaxing oil with
floral scent

- Fragrant smells, like flowers and flowery perfumes
- Woody smells, line pine trees or green grass
- Chemical smells, like bleach or ammonia
- Sweet smells, like chocolates with caramel centers
- Peppermint smells, like eucalyptus cough drops

- Nutty or toasty smells, like peanut butter or freshly popped popcorn
- Pungent smells, like strong cigar smoke or ripe blue cheese
- Decaying smells, like meat that is spoiled or mold
- Some smells don't fall into an exact category, but might be a combination of several categories. Of course, everyone's sense of smell is slightly different. Some people don't like to eat pungent cheese, because they don't like the smell of it.

When you smell spoiled meat

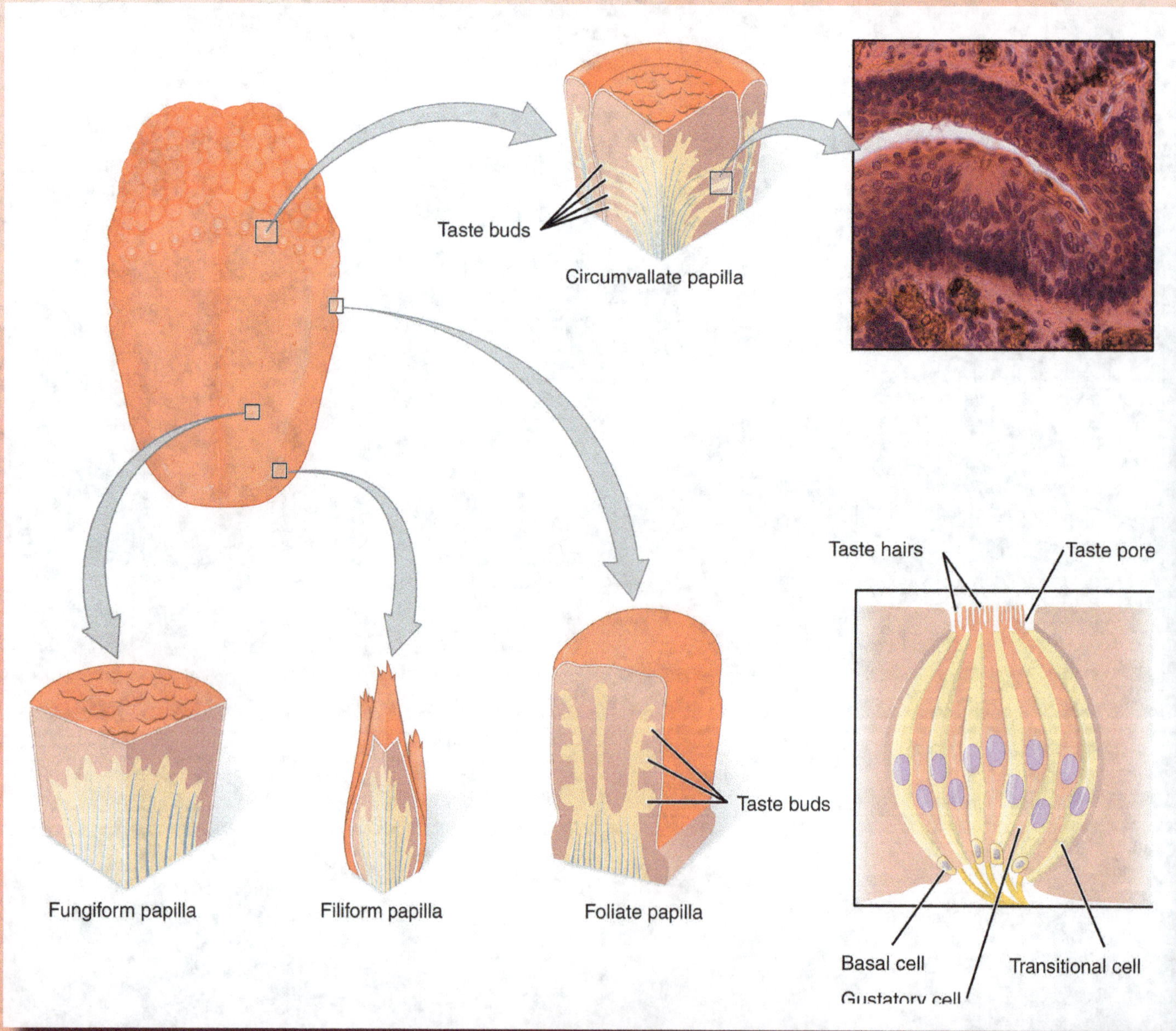

The structure of a tongue

THE STRUCTURE OF THE TONGUE

The tongue is a group of muscles in your mouth. When you lick an ice cream cone you use your tongue. When you talk or sing a song, you use your tongue.

When you chew up your food and then swallow it, you need your tongue too. You also need to use your tongue when you taste your food.

The flexible front part of your tongue moves around quite a bit. Working with your teeth and your voice it helps you to say words. The front part of your tongue also helps you while you're eating.

It tastes the food and it also moves the food around to the proper places in your mouth. It does this so your teeth can chew the food and grind it up, before it travels down to your stomach.

Tongue helps you pronounce the letters and words properly.

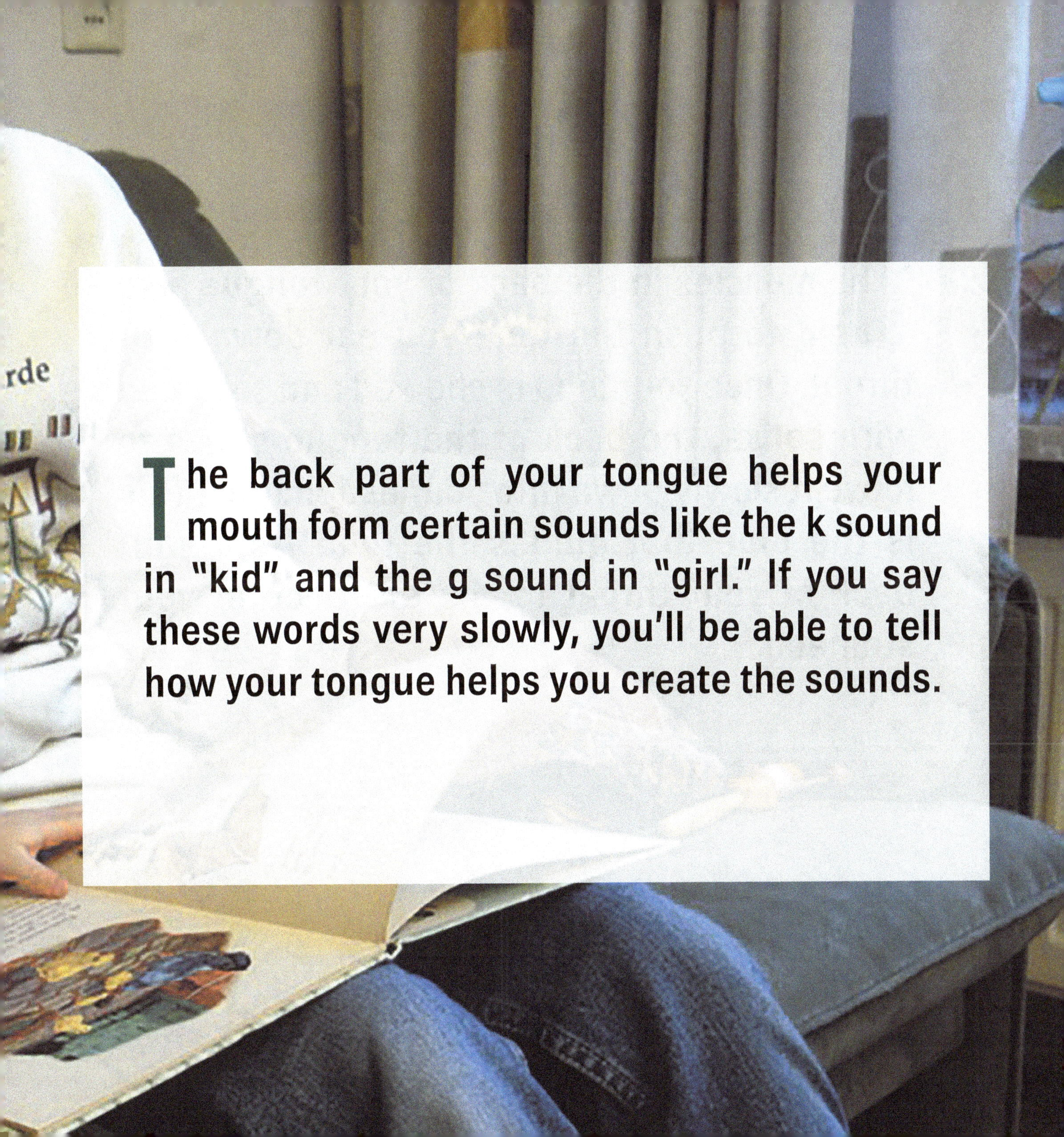

The back part of your tongue helps your mouth form certain sounds like the k sound in "kid" and the g sound in "girl." If you say these words very slowly, you'll be able to tell how your tongue helps you create the sounds.

The muscles in the back of your tongue also help to push the food you eat down your throat. Once your food is chewed and softened with saliva, the back of the tongue starts to move it slowly down into your esophagus. This is the pipe that guides the food from your back of your throat to the entrance of your stomach.

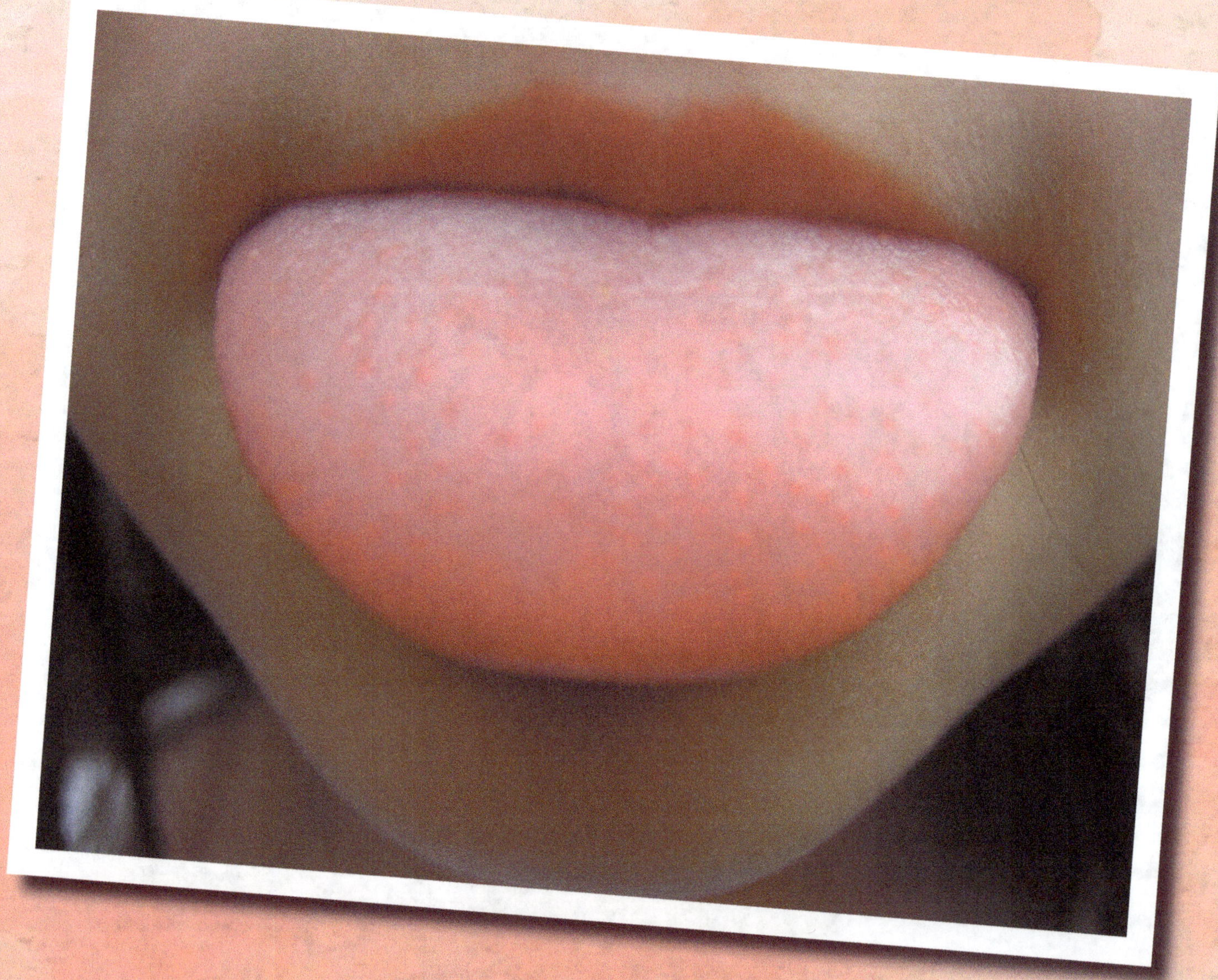

Tongue

WHAT ARE TASTE BUDS?

If you look at your tongue with a magnifying mirror, you'll see that its surface is very bumpy. Those bumps are the papillae. The papillae help the food stay in place and also move it into different positions as you chew.

These bumps also contain your taste receptors, which are called taste buds. When you're born, you have 10,000 or more of these taste buds. As you get older, your taste buds die out. Older people may have as few as 5,000 taste buds.

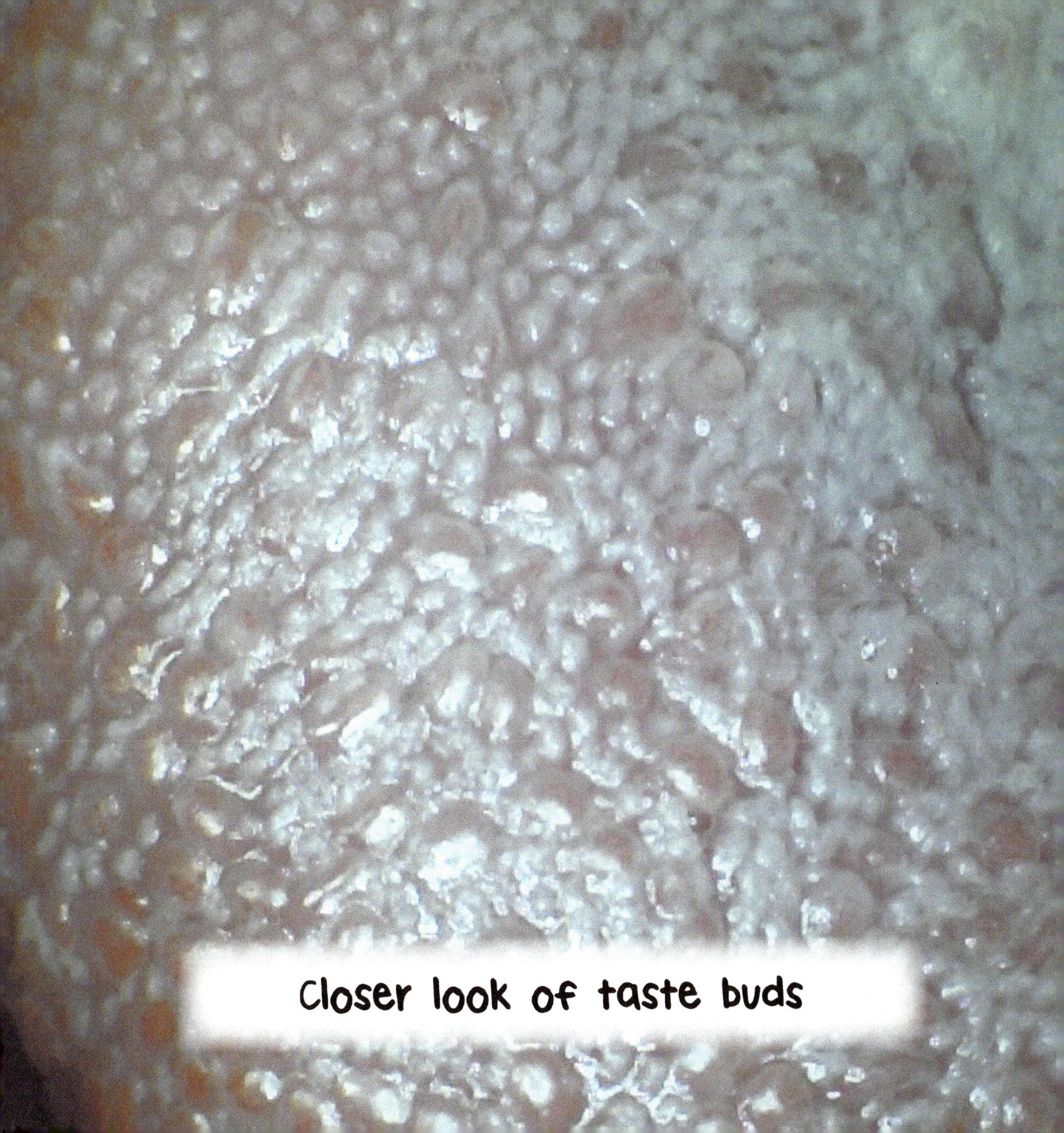
Closer look of taste buds

Just like with your nose, the taste buds contain tiny hairs that can only be seen with a microscope. They are microvilli and they send signals to your brain so you know what you're tasting. Your taste buds can tell whether something is sour like a lemon, sweet like a chocolate, bitter like dark leafy greens, or salty like a pretzel.

Scientists thought at one time that only certain areas of the tongue could taste certain flavors, but that's not true. You can taste any of the flavors anywhere on your tongue. It's pleasurable to taste foods, but your tongue also helps keep you safe. Part of the function of the taste buds is to tell you if something tastes strange and is unsafe to eat like milk that's spoiled.

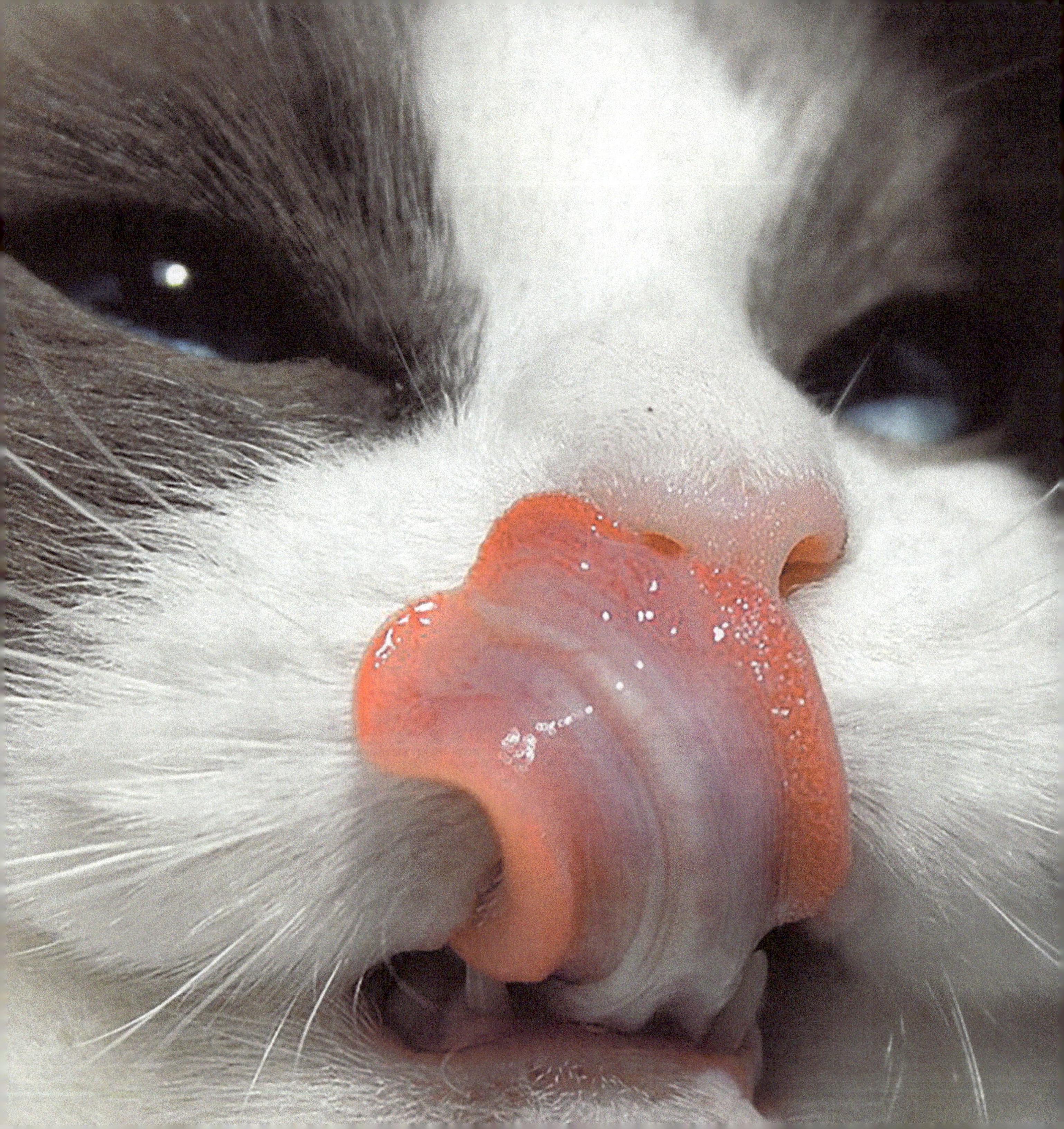

SMELL AND TASTE WORK TOGETHER

Smell and taste work together as two of our five senses. Have you ever noticed that when you have a cold, things don't taste good at all? This is due to the fact that smell and taste work together.

When you have a cold and you're all clogged up, then you can't really taste as well as you would normally because you can't smell too well. Strong smells can actually confuse your taste buds into tasting something differently than it should taste.

Less appetite

For example, if you hold a slice of strong onion under your nose while you're eating a sweet banana, the smell of the onion will probably make the banana taste different. Cold foods and icy drinks can dull your taste buds and so will very hot or very spicy foods.

Awesome! Now you know more about the senses of smell and taste. You can find more Biology books from Baby Professor by searching the website of your favorite book retailer.

Visit
BABY PROFESSOR
EDUCATION KIDS
www.BabyProfessorBooks.com
to download Free Baby Professor eBooks and view our catalog of new and exciting Children's Books

www.ingramcontent.com/pod-product-compliance
Lightning Source LLC
LaVergne TN
LVHW060828170826
845678LV00010B/1930

9798869431073